A
Pocket
Guide
to

O'AHU

text by **Curt Sanburn**
photography by **Douglas Peebles**

MUTUAL PUBLISHING

Library of Congress Catalog Card
Number: 00-100524

First Printing, August 2000
1 2 3 4 5 6 7 8 9

Design by Jane Hopkins

ISBN 1-56647-157-5

Mutual Publishing
1215 Center Street, Suite 210
Honolulu, Hawaii 96816
Telephone (808) 732-1709
Fax (808) 734-4094
e-mail: mutual@lava.net
www.mutualpublishing.com

Printed in Thailand

TABLE OF CONTENTS

KAHUKU POINT

TURTLE BAY

SUNSET BEACH
'Ehukai Beach Park

KAHUKU

Malaekahana Bay
State Recreation Area

LA'IE

WAIMEA BAY

Polynesian
Cultural Center

Waimea Falls Park

LANIAKEA BEACH

HAU'ULA

Hale'iwa Beach Park

Sacred Falls
State Park

WAIALUA   HALE'IWA

PUNALU'U

KA'ENA
POINT   MOKULE'IA

Dillingham
Airfield

Kahana Valley
State Park

Makua-Ka'ena
State Park

Ch
(M

MAKUA

Dole Pineapple
Pavilion

Kea'au Beach Park

MT. KA'ALA

WAHIAWA

KA

Schofield
Barracks

Makaha Beach Park   MAKAHA

MILILANI

WAI'ANAE

Poka'i Bay Beach Park

PEARL CITY

MA'ILI

WAIPAHU

AIEA

MA'ILI POINT   NANAKULI

Nanakuli Beach Park

PEARL HARBOR

Kahe Point Beach Park   MAKAKILO

'EWA

Honolulu
International
Airport

Campbell
Industrial
Park   Barbers Point
Naval Air Station

'EWA BEACH

H

One'ula
Beach Park

Sand Island

BARBERS POINT

Honolulu Harbor

Downtown Honolulu

O‘AHU
FACTS & FIGURES

County: City and County of Honolulu
Land area: 600.2 square miles (1995)
Resident population: 870,761 (1995)
Highest point: Mt. Ka‘ala, 4,003 feet
Shoreline: 112 miles
Extreme length and width: 44 miles by 30 miles
Average annual temperature: 76.8°F (1995)
Highest recorded temperature: 95°F, Honolulu
   International Airport (1998)
Lowest recorded temperature: 53°F, Honolulu
   International Airport (1998)
Average annual rainfall at Honolulu Airport :
   23 inches
Average annual rainfall at Manoa Valley:
   (about 7 miles from the airport): 158 inches
Chief industries: tourism, construction, defense,
   imported oil
Energy sources: 95% from imported oil
Hotel and condominium rental units: 36,206
   (1998)
Visitors per year: 4,718,420 (1998)
Average number of visitors per day: 77,020
   (1997)
Public and private golf courses: 39
Public tennis courts: 201 (1995)
State Parks: 31
County Parks: 291 (1996)
National Parks: 1
Recognized surfing sites: 594

THE MASSIVE WHITE FRONT OF THE SHERATON
HOTEL, THE PINK OASIS OF THE ROYAL HAWAIIAN
HOTEL, AND THE TWIN TOWERS OF THE HYATT
REGENCY HOTEL DOMINATE THE MODERN
OUTLINE OF WAIKIKI'S BEACHFRONT.

INTRODUCTION

THE HAWAI'I LOA, A REPLICA OF AN ANCIENT POLYNESIAN VOYAGING CANOE, SAILS INTO KANE'OHE BAY ON THE WINDWARD COAST OF O'AHU. THIS SEAFARING VESSEL, BUILT ACCORDING TO ANCIENT DESIGN, IS USED TO TEST THEORIES OF THE EARLY HAWAIIAN MIGRATIONS AND NAVIGATIONAL TECHNIQUES.

❋ ❋ ❋ ❋ ❋

WELCOME TO THE ISLAND of O'ahu, where Polynesia meets the twenty-first century—and both win. Nowhere in Hawai'i are the contemporary realities and complexities of life in paradise more vivid: the booming prosperity, the cultural and racial confluences, the proud history, the trade-offs between preservation and progress ... all of it played out against a spectacular natural beauty.

The simplest images express it best: Honolulu's glittering high-rises crowded between a blue sea and emerald mountains; freeway traffic cooled by soft trade winds and gilded by blazing sunsets; the stunning regularity of rainbows arched over both the city and its outlying plains.

Honolulu and its Waikiki resort district usually overwhelm any other impression of the island. However, the great surprise to most visitors is how spectacular the rest of O'ahu is, both physically and socially.

Topographically, this 600-square-mile mature volcanic island is the most varied and intimate of the major Hawaiian islands. Spread out along O'ahu's four distinct coastlines like a dreamer's checklist of tropical essentials are coral reefs, sheltered lagoons, scores of beaches, broad, well-defined bays, view-perfect promontories, mist-shrouded valleys, dry leeward plains, and sheer velvet cliffs. **Note:** Directions in Hawaiian are not given in familiar terms of North, South, East and West. In Honolulu, "Diamond Head" means toward that landmark, "'Ewa" means toward that town, or West. Otherwise *mauka* means "toward the mountains," and *makai* means "toward the sea."

The stretching Ko'olau mountain range to the east and the Wai'anae range to the west, with a broad central plain in between, define the island. The 4,000-foot peaks, sloping ridges and steep-walled *pali* (cliffs) are the remains of the much higher Ko'olau and Wai'anae volcanoes that emerged from the Pacific about three million years ago. On O'ahu, nature has had plenty of time to rearrange its crude volcanoes into a magical landscape. Eons of stream and wave erosion have carried much of the original mass back into the sea, leaving behind the soft, deeply folded draperies of Windward O'ahu and the alternating valleys and ridges that provide Honolulu's dramatic backdrop. Later volcanic activity added the finishing touch with a series of volcanic cones: the beloved landmarks—Diamond Head, Punchbowl, and Koko Head.

O'ahu has been known as "the gathering place" since ancient days, when chiefs from the other, more populous islands conferred at Waikiki, which was then neutral ground.

THE CONCRETE MASS OF HONOLULU'S HIGH-RISES BELLIES UP TO THE BLUE OCEAN BEYOND THE GROOVED GREEN OF THE KO'OLAU MOUNTAINS. THIS STARK CONTRAST OF NATURAL BEAUTY AND MAN-MADE GEOMETRY IS CONSISTENTLY REPLAYED THROUGHOUT THE ISLAND OF O'AHU.

✳   ✳   ✳

O'ahu's modern history begins in late 1794, sixteen years after British Captain James Cook found and named the Sandwich Islands. A British fur trading ship, *Jackal*, inched through a break in the coral reef protecting a small O'ahu fishing village called Kou and found a commodious harbor that the sailors named Fair Haven—"Honolulu" in Hawaiian. The promise of a safe anchorage and nearby fresh water and food (and, no doubt, its exotic name) drew adventurers, sandalwood traders, merchants and whalers from America and Europe to Honolulu. New England Protestant missionaries quickly followed—to remind the sailors-away-from-home of their spiritual responsibilities, and to clothe and convert the Hawaiians. By 1850, when King Kamehameha III relocated the royal capital here from Lahaina, Maui, Honolulu was a bustling Pacific port-of-call.

As the city grew, its wealthy residents sought refuge from the dust, heat and overdressed fussiness of Victorian Honolulu. They found it two miles away at Waikiki, a traditional surfing and fishing beach reserved for O'ahu's *ali'i*. Hawai'i's royalty built

Catamarans with rainbow sails skirt the waves rolling toward Waikiki's shore. On the distant point, at the base of majestic Diamond Head, lies a cluster of buildings, the posh retreat known as the "Gold Coast."

modest cottages there, in the ancient coconut groves at Helumoa, where the Royal Hawaiian Hotel now stands. Western businessmen followed and soon learned from the Hawaiians how to surf the gentle waves. In 1901, the first modern hotel at Waikiki, the Moana, opened. Its first guests were 100 visiting Shriners.

Today, the island has more than 840,000 residents, representing 80 percent of Hawai'i's one-million-plus population. On any given day it hosts about 75,000 visitors. Honolulu is the state capital, by far its largest city, and headquarters for banking, construction, transportation, agriculture, manufacturing, and tourism. The U.S. Army, Navy, and Air Force commands based on O'ahu involve more than 116,000 military personnel and their dependents, and control one quarter of O'ahu's land area.

The City and County of Honolulu —a single political entity—covers the entire island; "Honolulu" usually refers to the urban swath along O'ahu's south shore from Koko Head in the east to Pearl Harbor in the west, and from the ocean into the Ko'olau mountains. Having their own distinct personalities are the bedroom communities of Kailua

A COLORFUL CANOE SETS OUT ACROSS CRYSTAL CLEAR WATERS IN THE "FAIR HAVEN" OF WAIKIKI.

✻   ✻   ✻

and Kane'ohe on the far side of the Ko'olau mountains; the sprawling commuter suburbs of 'Aiea, Pearl City, Waipahu, 'Ewa, and Mililani to the west; the military centers at Pearl Harbor, Hickam Air Force Base, Barbers Point Naval Air Station, Wheeler Air Force Base, and the U.S. Army Schofield Barracks; and the rural coastal communities of Wai'anae, Waialua, Hale'iwa, Kahuku, La'ie, Kahalu'u and Waimanalo.

Slightly more than half of the people on O'ahu were born in Hawai'i and call themselves kama'aina, children of the land. The rest, malihini, moved here. Thirty-three percent of the total population is Caucasian or haole. Another 21 percent are first-, second-, third-, or fourth-generation Japanese: issei, nisei, sansei, or yonsei. Hawaiians or part-Hawaiians constitute 18 percent. The remaining 28 percent include Filipinos, Chinese, Portuguese, Samoans, Koreans, Tongans, Vietnamese, Cambodians, African-Americans, and Puerto Ricans, in that order of significance. Nearly half of O'ahu's marriages are interracial.

This color blindness, this hospitality, is the legacy of the Hawaiian people. From the moment of first

contact with Europeans in 1778, the Hawaiians were open-armed. Tragically, the cost of *aloha* was devastating, as introduced diseases, economic exploitation, and political conquest brought the Hawaiians to the edge of extinction.

Somehow the spirit of *aloha* prevailed, and the Hawaiian host-culture is still the touchstone for almost every aspect of Hawai'i's uniqueness: the racial harmony, graceful way of life, famous music and dance, colorful integration of nature into man-made things, and stewardship of the *'aina,* the land.

Despite intensive land and golf course developments, O'ahu's pleasures are the same today as yesterday. The trade winds continue to blow and the pure colors of the mountains and the sea continue to amaze. Honolulu is still, by any measure, a glamorous, glorious city. Every day its golden people prove the remarkable durability of the *aloha* spirit, that guileless local friendliness that transcends the realities of workaday life.

✳   ✳   ✳   ✳   ✳

KAILUA BEACH ON THE WINDWARD SIDE OF O'AHU IS AN IDYLLIC SPOT FOR SUNBATHERS AND WATER ENTHUSIASTS ALIKE.

Towering above the central plains of Oʻahu, and
stretching from Kaʻena Point to ʻEwa, the
Waiʻanae Mountains are what remains of the
older of two volcanoes that created the island.
Kolekole Pass, the shallow declivity in this range,
marks the flight path the Japanese "zeros" used in
their attack on Pearl Harbor.

VIGNETTES

King Sugar

Brought to Hawai'i as a food plant by the Polynesians, sugar cane, a giant grass, was first planted commercially in 1802. The enterprise failed but some forty years later, the California Gold Rush and the American Civil War spurred demand for sugar, and large plantations on former chiefly and royal lands sprang up on all the islands. The new landowners were *haole,* the Caucasian sons of missionaries or adventurous sailors who made Hawai'i their home. The planters became the *ali'i,* Hawai'i's ruling class, and eventually overthrew the Hawaiian monarchy. A reciprocity treaty with the U.S. eliminated import duties on Hawaiian sugar. By 1890, Hawai'i was exporting 250 million pounds of sugar a year.

Adequate labor was the planters' big problem. Hawaiians, besides being ravaged by disease, did not like plantation life. The plantation owners looked to China then to the Portuguese islands of Madeira and the Azores, and Japan, Korea, and the Philippines. Between

SOME OF THE LAST SUGAR FIELDS ON O'AHU STRETCH ACROSS THE ISLAND'S ISTHMUS. THE WAIALUA SUGAR MILL ENDED AN ERA WHEN ITS EQUIPMENT WAS SHUT DOWN FOR THE FINAL TIME IN THE FALL OF 1996.

1852 and 1948, roughly 350,000 contract workers arrived in Hawai'i to work the twenty-seven plantations spread across most of Hawai'i's arable land. Many stayed after their contracts were up to form the basis of a new multi-cultural society. Although the plantations have dwindled, the descendants of the workers have flourished.

Hawai'i's old plantation camps were historically akin to New York's Ellis Island—places where immigrants had their first taste of life in a strange and wonderful new land.

MISSION HOUSES MUSEUM, NEXT TO KAWAIAHA'O CHURCH, INCLUDES THE OLDEST WESTERN BUILDINGS IN HAWAI'I. HERE EACH SATURDAY A "LIVING HISTORY" PROGRAM OF COSTUMED ACTORS DEPICTS LIFE IN OLD HONOLULU.

✻   ✻   ✻

New England Sailors vs. New England Missionaries

By the early 1820s, Hawai'i had a reputation among merchant sailors as a mid-ocean paradise where the native women were enthusiastic and open-armed. New England's church leaders thought it a place of heathen licentiousness and defilement. The first group of Congregational missionaries sailed from Boston in 1820. They quickly converted the royal families in Lahaina and Honolulu to Christianity and taught them to read. Much distressed by the wanton exploitation and infection of young Hawaiian women by diseased sailors, the missionaries encouraged the chiefs to pass laws prohibiting the local women from visiting foreign ships.

In 1826, when the USS *Dolphin* arrived in Honolulu, the captain demanded that women be allowed to board his ship despite the new laws. The Queen Regent, Ka'ahumanu, refused, for which the ship's captain quickly blamed the influential Rev. Hiram Bingham, the leader of the Honolulu mission. On a Sunday afternoon, a gang of *Dolphin* sailors rioted in Honolulu, breaking the precious glass windows of the Queen's grass house and threatening Bingham. The missionary was probably saved from a thrashing when a group of club-swinging Hawaiians rushed to his aid. Finally, the Reverend had to restrain his ardent defenders, who were intent on bashing out the brains of the overpowered sailors.

As with most confrontations between Hawaiians and foreigners, the chiefs and their missionary allies were

THE SEAL OF THE KINGDOM OF HAWAI'I GRACES THE WROUGHT-IRON GATES THAT PROTECT THE ENTRANCE TO KING LUNALILO'S MAUSOLEUM.

THREE HISTORIC STRUCTURES BUILT BETWEEN 1821 AND 1841 ARE ON DISPLAY AT THE MISSION HOUSE MUSEUM.

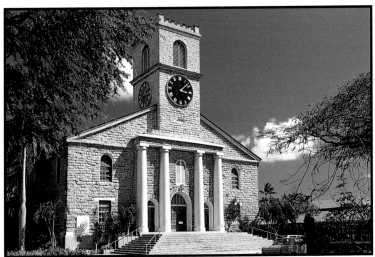

KAWAIAHA'O CONGREGATIONAL CHURCH WAS COMPLETED IN 1840 AFTER A DECADE OF CONSTRUCTION THAT USED 14,000 LARGE CORAL BLOCKS.

forced to back down when *Dolphin's* captain threatened military action against the kingdom if his demands were not met. A day after the riot, boatloads of women went out to the waiting American warship.

Hawaiian Hospitality, circa 1873

"As for the common people, they are by nature or long custom, or both, as kindly and hospitable as men can be. If you ask for lodgings at night-fall at a native hut, you are received as though you were conferring a favor; frequently the whole house, which has but one room, is set apart for you, the people going elsewhere to sleep; a chicken is slain in your honor and for your exclusive supper; and you are served by the master of the house himself."

—*Charles Nordhoff,
describing his 1873
visit to Hawai'i*

AUNTIES, OR *TUTU*, LIKE THIS HAPPY LADY WITH HER 'UKULELE, STRUM AND SING THEIR WAY THROUGH COUNTLESS HAWAIIAN SONGS AT FESTIVALS AND PARTIES ALL OVER THE ISLAND. THE COSTUME—A LOOSE—FITTING, BRIGHT FLORAL *MU'UMU'U* ACCENTUATED BY A *LEI*, A STRAW HAT WITH HAT *LEI*, AND A FLOWER BEHIND THE EAR—HAS BECOME AS CHARACTERISTIC OF THESE FOLK BANDS AS THEIR SWEET FALSETTO VOICES.

❊　　　❊　　　❊

Hawaiian Impression

"No alien land in all the world has any deep strong charm for me but that one, no other land could so longingly and so beseechingly haunt me, sleeping and waking, through half a lifetime, as that one has done. Other things leave me, but it abides; other things change, but it remains the same. For me its balmy airs are always blowing, its summer seas flashing in the sun; the pulsing of its surfbeat is in my ear; I can see its garlanded crags, its leaping cascades, its plumy palms drowsing by the shore, its remote summits floating like islands above the cloud rack; I can feel the spirit of its woodland solitudes, I can hear the splash of its brooks; in my nostrils still lives the breath of flowers that perished twenty years ago."

—*Mark Twain*

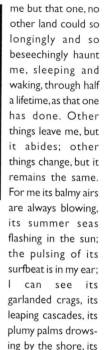

The Dole Pineapple Company cultivates these fields in the broad midsection of the island of O'ahu.

This fruit stand in the Manoa Valley is one of many locally-owned ventures that supply delicious produce to small businesses and residents throughout the island.

ON SOME DAYS, FROM THE RUGGED TIP OF KA'ENA POINT YOU CAN WATCH RAIN CURTAINS CATCH ALONG THE SLOPES TO THE LEFT WHILE SUNSHINE BATHES THE WAI'ANAE COAST ON THE RIGHT.

NATURAL SPECTACLES

MYTHOLOGY NOTWITHSTANDING, THE 1,600-mile-long chain of Hawaiian islands was built by volcanic action beginning roughly 30 million years ago at Kure Atoll, now at the north-western end of the archipelago, and continuing today on and near the Big Island at the southeastern end of the chain. A slow, steady northwestern drift of the earth's upper layer over a deep "hot spot" accounts for the island chain's linear shape and the progressive age of the islands within the chain.

The chain's major landform is the broadly rounded "shield" volcano, built up by innumerable thin lava flows from the ocean floor to heights exceeding two miles above sea level. Mauna Loa on the Big Island is a classic—and still active—shield volcano, so gentle in its rise that its 13,600-foot height above sea level (as high as most Rocky Mountain peaks) is difficult to comprehend.

On the eight major islands, it's easy to see the geological evolution from the broad, swelling shapes of young and intact shield volcanoes on the Big Island to the heavily eroded, jagged topography of Kaua'i and, finally, to the low-lying, almost completely worn-down remains of an even older shield volcano on Ni'ihau.

The three-million-year-old island of O'ahu is older than both Maui and the Big Island, but younger than Kaua'i. There is extreme erosion on O'ahu's windward side but more moderate erosion in its central valley, where the Wai'anae and Ko'olau ranges retain some of their original volcanic shape.

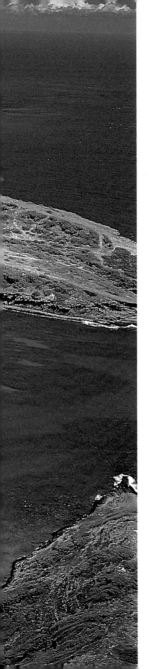

The effects of rainfall and its resulting stream erosion are most striking on the rainy, windward northeastern sides of all islands. Windward O'ahu, with its near-vertical cliffs and broad valleys, has been so completely transformed by stream action that the shape and size of the original Ko'olau shield volcano is very difficult to imagine. In contrast, the leeward slopes, receiving much less rainfall, show relatively little stream erosion.

Marine erosion is most apparent on windward shores. Wind-driven waves have carved low, jagged sea cliffs at O'ahu's southeast corner between Hanauma Bay and Sandy Beach, and at Makapu'u Point. (Sea cliffs as high as 3,000 feet define the north shore of Moloka'i, among the highest sea cliffs in the world.)

Sedimentation and reef construction, plus changes in sea level over millions of years, account for Hawai'i's few real "plains," most notably along the southwestern shores of O'ahu. Other land-shaping forces include earthquakes, wind, and, of course, man-made environs.

✻   ✻   ✻   ✻   ✻

HANAUMA BAY WAS ONCE A FAVORITE RETREAT FOR HAWAIIAN ROYALTY. TODAY THE 101–ACRE EXPANSE OF CRYSTALLINE BLUE WATER WITHIN THIS REMNANT OF A VOLCANIC CRATER IS A STATE MARINE LIFE CONSERVATION DISTRICT. A PROTECTED REEF TEEMING WITH FISH PROVIDES SOME OF HAWAI'I'S BEST SNORKELING AND DIVING. THE LARGE SAND-BOTTOM HOLES IN THE CORAL ARE THE WORK OF AMERICAN GI'S STATIONED HERE ON BEACH DEFENSE DURING WORLD WAR II. TO GIVE THEMSELVES A PLACE TO SWIM THE SOLDIERS TOSSED GRENADES INTO THE WATER AND BLEW UP THE REEF.

THE HIKE ALONG THE HEAVILY-VEGETATED SUMMIT OF THE KOʻOLAU MOUNTAIN RANGE OFFERS VIEWS OF CITY AND COUNTRY, AGRICULTURE AND INDUSTRY. THE FOOTING IS SOMETIMES DANGEROUS, BUT THE VIEW IS WORTH THE RISKS.

The white sands of Kailua Beach Park cut like a bright beam of light between the bay's placid blue waters and the forest-cloaked Ko'olau Mountains.

Left: Legend says that Hi'iaka, goddess of the forests, journeyed north through the island chain to fetch a young man named Lohiau from his home on Kaua'i. At Kualoa, on the island of O'ahu, she was attacked by Mokoli'i, a huge evil lizard. In the ensuing battle, she cut off his tail and tossed it into the sea. The tail became the islet known today as Chinaman's Hat.

MOST SURFERS SAY THE SAME THING: RIDING THE
MOUNTAINOUS WAVES OF WAIMEA BAY IS THE ULTIMATE
TEST OF A WATERMAN'S COURAGE, AND THE GREATEST
THRILL IN SPORTS.

TOURS

THE WINDWARD COAST & NORTH SHORE

THIS ISLAND HALF-CIRCLE covers O'ahu's most popular scenery and beaches in a single, long drive. A full day in the car, allowing some time for several short stops along the way, will orient you to most of eastern, northern, and central O'ahu's charms; you can then decide what to revisit on another day.

Assuming you're in Waikiki, drive east on Kalakaua Avenue, around the seaward side of Diamond Head into residential East Honolulu. Beginning with Kahala, Honolulu's most expensive suburb, the neighborhoods line up along Kalaniana'ole Highway like an array of gardens. Some, like Wai'alae Nui, Wai'alae Iki, and Hawai'i Loa, climb the ridges for mile-high views of Maunalua Bay. Others, like 'Aina Koa, 'Aina Haina, Niu Valley, and Kuli'ou'ou stretch from placid reef-front shores to distinctive deep valleys. The vast suburban development at Hawai'i Kai, with shopping centers, winding inshore lagoon, and marina, lies in the shadow of Koko Head and Koko Crater.

Hawai'i Kai is the easternmost reach of residential Honolulu. Just a half mile beyond the Koko Marina Shopping center is the entrance to Hanauma Bay Beach Park. This famed and very crowded spot is a deep circular bay formed when one side of a volcanic crater collapsed into the sea. Drive into the parking area and walk over to the lookout for the view.

Beyond the bay is the dramatic southeast coastline of O'ahu, dominated by the craggy, surf-battered cliffs of Koko Crater and spectacular views across Kaiwi

Channel to the islands of Moloka'i and Lana'i. (On a clear day, you might see 10,000-foot Haleakala on Maui behind the long, low-slung west end of Moloka'i.) There are several scenic lookouts along the winding two-lane highway. All are worthwhile stops.

The road straightens at Sandy Beach (see Beaches) and continues past

A SNORKELER KICKS DEEPER TO EXPLORE THE MARINE LIFE IN KANE'OHE BAY.

✻   ✻   ✻

some wide-open undeveloped beach front to Makapu'u Point. The sunny golf course on the *mauka* side of the highway is the thirty-six-hole Hawai'i Kai Championship Course, designed by Robert Trent Jones (open to the public). At Makapu'u lookout the highway turns O'ahu's southeast corner for a breathtaking introduction to the deeply-folded mountains, bright beaches, and offshore islands of the windward side.

Directly below the lookout is Makapu'u Beach (see Beaches), a famous bodysurfing spot and O'ahu's most dramatic cove. When the winds are steady, hang-gliders launch themselves off the 2,000-foot cliffs and soar for hours on the trade-wind updrafts. At the foot of the cliffs is Sea Life Park, a very successful educational marine museum featuring trained dolphins, whales, sea lions, and penguins

in splashy, regularly scheduled shows; a whaling museum; and a 300,000-gallon glass Hawaiian Reef Tank that puts you up-close-and-personal with some 2,000 different denizens of Hawai'i's deep, including a creepy-looking hammerhead shark. Across the road, deep-sea oceanographic, marine biology, and aquaculture research is carried out from Makai Pier.

Follow Kalaniana'ole Highway to rural Waimanalo, where the unbelievable background *pali* (cliffs) drop in sheer, velvety folds to rich ranchlands and farms of banana, papaya, anthuriums, corn, lettuce, and other produce. A quick side tour into one of Waimanalo's back roads (Kumuhau Street, just north of town, is best) provides a glimpse of O'ahu's rapidly disappearing small-scale, rural way of life.

The wide and safe beachfront is accessible from the Waimanalo Bay Recreational Center and Waimanalo Beach Park (see Beaches).

North of Waimanalo, past the peak of Mt. Olomana on the left, passage through the bedroom communities of Kailua and Kane'ohe requires two separate jogs. From Kalaniana'ole Highway (72) turn left on Pali Highway

During the summer, Makapu'u Beach on the southeastern tip of the island of O'ahu is a popular local surf spot. Watch out for the lifeguard's red flags signaling dangerous rip tides that blast into the cove.

Sunday afternoons on the Sand Bar in Kane'ohe Bay require a minus tide, a colorful sail, lawn chairs, a picnic lunch, and 45 sunblock.

A cul-de-sac of ocean treasures, Hanauma Bay was formed when the seaward wall of an ancient volcanic crater collapsed. Its name is appropriate—*hana* means bay, and *uma* is curved.

(61) in front of Castle Memorial Hospital; after two miles, hang a right onto Kamehameha Highway (83) into Kane'ohe. The Pali public golf course is on the left beneath the cloud-shrouded Nu'uanu *pali,* and private Hawai'i Loa College is on the right. The view of broad Kane'ohe Bay opens up, with the hangars of Kane'ohe Marine Corps Air Station clearly visible on Mokapu Peninsula beyond. Past Kane'ohe town, the highway narrows again to two lanes and resumes its tour of rural O'ahu, starting with quiet bayside He'eia. The shady gardens at Heeia State Park overlook O'ahu's largest ancient fishpond.

THE BYODO-IN TEMPLE WAS BUILT IN 1968. THIS REPLICA OF A FAMOUS KYOTO TEMPLE HOUSES A THREE-TON BRONZE BELL AND AN 18-FOOT-HIGH BUDDHA.

✻ ✻ ✻

A left turn at the landmark Hygienic Store in Kahalu'u will take you two miles to the Valley of the Temples Memorial Park, a non-denominational cemetery of extraordinary beauty. The Byodo-In Temple there is an exact replica of a 900-year-old temple in Kyoto, Japan. Set amid carp ponds and Japanese gardens with the deeply-fluted Ko'olau *pali* as a backdrop, this quiet Buddhist temple is meant for meditation.

After your visit, return to the Hygienic Store and continue northward on Kamehameha Highway through the lush bay-front Kahalu'u, Waiahole, and Waikane areas. Roadside stands sell papayas, bananas, coconuts, and juices from nearby valley farms. Kualoa Regional Park, to the right where the highway re-emerges on the coast, is worth a stop for stunning views of the Ko'olaus, Kane'ohe Bay and little Mokoli'i Island, "Chinaman's Hat." Northward, the highway runs along a quiet, reef-protected stretch of sandy beachfront past rural Ka'a'awa, Punalu'u, Hau'ula, and La'ie. Great undeveloped valleys alternate with muscular mountain ridges plunging right down to the sea. The windy, salt-sprayed Ko'olauloa district gets plenty of rain. Heavy downpours lace the steep mountainsides with silvery waterfalls. This lush, bountiful area is home to many Hawaiians and other Polynesians, who fish the reefs and grow bananas and *taro* in the valleys. Lovely Kahana Bay, with a fine beach, ancient fishpond, coconut grove, winding stream and deep valley (one of the wettest spots on the island), is good for a picnic ... or a nap.

At La'ie is the Polynesian Cultural Center, Hawai'i's most popular paid visitor attraction. Established by the Mormon Church, which has its Pacific headquarters in La'ie, the center is a

SUGAR, ONCE THE MOST POWERFUL INDUSTRY IN HAWAI'I, HAS BEEN COMPLETELY PHASED OUT ON THE ISLAND OF O'AHU. THIS MILL, IN THE SMALL COMMUNITY OF KAHUKU NEAR THE NORTHERN MOST TIP OF THE ISLAND, STANDS AS A MEMORIAL TO THOSE GLORY DAYS OF KING SUGAR.

CLIFF DIVERS HURL THEMSELVES OVER THE 45-FOOT WAIMEA FALLS ON THE NORTH SHORE EACH AFTERNOON TO WOW THE VISITORS TO THIS 1,800-ACRE BOTANICAL GARDEN.

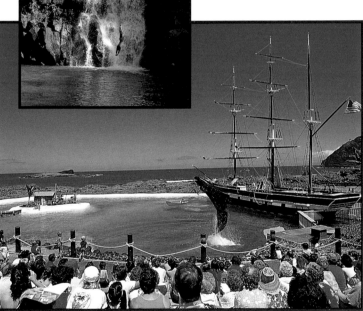

SEA LIFE PARK IS A 62-ACRE OCEAN THEME PARK, WHERE FALSE KILLER WHALES, PORPOISES, PENGUINS, AND SEALS PIROUETTE, CLAP, AND LEAP THROUGH HOOPS IN AN ARENA-AQUARIUM. HUNDREDS OF DIFFERENT MARINE ANIMALS ARE ALSO ON DISPLAY IN A GIANT 3,000-GALLON REEF TANK.

collection of re-created native villages representing the seven island cultures of Polynesia: Hawaiian, Samoan, Tahitian, Maori, Fijian, Marquesan, and Tongan. The displays and demonstrations are fascinating and informative. Most of the extremely friendly guides and performers are students from the various islands at the nearby Brigham Young University -Hawai'i campus. Plan to spend at least a half-day here, particularly if you want to learn about Hawai'i's Polynesian cousins. The center is closed on Sundays.

Beaches in this area include the lovely, but unfortunately named, "Pounders" between Hau'ula and La'ie; Hukilau Beach, across the highway and just north of the Mormon Temple in La'ie; and Malaekahana State Recreation Area north of La'ie.

At the northeastern corner of the island, the old plantation town of Kahuku marks the beginning of O'ahu's famed North Shore. The broad plains in this area were once a sandalwood forest, levelled in the early nineteenth century for the lucrative China trade. From 1880 to 1971, sugarcane was king, as evidenced by the impressive Kahuku Sugar Mill, now shut down and converted into tourist shops. Some of

NOTHING BEATS MATSUMOTO SHAVE ICE AFTER MAKING THE LONG TREK FROM HONOLULU TO THE NORTH SHORE TOWN OF HALE'IWA. FINE ICE SHAVINGS PLACED IN A CONICAL PAPER CUP ARE DOUSED WITH PINEAPPLE, COCONUT, STRAWBERRY, ORANGE, OR VANILLA SYRUP. WHAT A TREAT!

✳   ✳   ✳

the old cane fields now grow corn, lettuce, papaya, and tomatoes; others are sprawling aqua-culture ponds. In the low hills above the Kameha-meha Highway, just beyond Kahuku, is a field of wind-driven generators —including the largest one in the world, with blades as long as the wings on a Boeing 747. All are testing this alternate source of energy for oil-dependent Honolulu.

Turtle Bay and neighboring Kawela Bay are now becoming a major resort center. The Turtle Bay Hilton and Country Club, on the northern most point of the island features the North Shore's only resort, the Turtle Bay Hilton, with two 18-hole golf courses, tennis, and horseback riding. Beyond, the famed surfing sites of the North Shore line up all the way to the town of Hale'iwa, ten miles down the coast: Velzyland, Sunset Point, Sunset, Rocky Point, Pupukea, Ehukai, Pipeline, Backdoors, Rock Piles, Waimea, Chun's Reef, Laniakea, Hale'iwa, and Ali'i.

Serving the hallowed surfing grounds is Sunset Beach, a funky, sandy settlement, really not much more than a pizza stand, two surf shops, a small grocery called Kammies, a screened restaurant selling plate lunches, and a gas station. This is true surfer atmosphere. You are in town (or you have arrived) when the houses thicken and the highway suddenly opens up to the Sunset Beach parking area and beach.

At the big Foodland supermarket in nearby Pupukea, turn left up Pupukea Road and take the first right turn to the Pu'u O Mahuka Heiau, O'ahu's largest and most nearly intact Hawaiian temple. Another perfect place for meditation, this ancient stone platform commands its Pacific Ocean view like a Greek temple.

THE WINDWARD COAST HAS BECOME A MECCA FOR WINDSURFERS, WHOSE FAVORITE RUNS LIE OFF KAILUA BEACH. IT'S ALSO A MECCA FOR SUNBATHERS.

✻   ✻   ✻

A half-mile beyond Pupukea Road, where the highway takes a deep curve around Waimea Bay, is the entrance to Waimea Falls Park, a popular attraction with an admission fee. The park features a botanical garden, demonstrations of ancient Hawaiian crafts and games, a cliff-diving show at Waimea Falls, and gift shops and dining. Waimea Valley itself was once a thriving Hawaiian settlement. The beach at Waimea Bay , like most on the North Shore, is fabulous for swimming in summer and spectacular for surf-watching in winter.

Continue on to Hale'iwa, a busy surf and boating town, where there is food and delicious "shave ice." If time permits, consider driving through the quaint plantation town of Waialua on to Mokule'ia for a look at the seaside polo fields—or for a glider ride at Dillingham Field.

The forty-five-minute drive back on Kamehameha Highway back to Honolulu rises through O'ahu's lofty Leilehua plain. At lower elevations, cane fields give way to pineapple. Much of the forest visible in the foothills to the east and west are training grounds and communications outposts for the U.S. Army, Navy, and Air Force.

The Dole Plantation Visitors Pavilion, just before the town of Wahiawa, beckons to pineapple lovers. Next door is Helemano Plantation, a delightful garden, restaurant, and giftshop operated by handicapped workers who demonstrate Hawaiian crafts, serve the food they've grown, and sell the gifts they've handcrafted.

Wahiawa is another old plantation town, now serving nearby Schofield Barracks, home of the 25th Light Infantry Division, and adjacent Wheeler Air Force Base. To the west, the low gap in the Wai'anae range is Kolekole Pass, through which Japanese planes slipped, undetected by radar, on their way to bomb Wheeler field, Hickam air field, and Pearl Harbor on December 7, 1941.

From Wahiawa, the H-2 Freeway descends from the central plain as the south shore of Oʻahu spreads out before you: the broad Ewa plain and Barber's Point to the west, Pearl Harbor and ever-advancing Waipahu and Pearl City to the south, while off in the eastern distance above a thicket of Honolulu high-rises is the unmistakable outline of Diamond Head. At Waipahu, the H-2 Freeway merges with H-1, which you'll follow into Honolulu.

The Puʻu O Mahuka Heiau, on the hill above Waimea Bay, is the largest intact Hawaiian temple on the island of Oʻahu. Used anciently as a place of worship and sacrifice, this stone enclosure remains sacred.

Right: A skimboarder sprints for a receding wave at Sandy Beach.

THE NU'UANU PALI LOOKOUT, PERHAPS THE MOST
WRITTEN-ABOUT SCENIC SPOT ON O'AHU, AFFORDS A
VERY CONVENIENT VIEW OF THE WINDWARD COAST.
THE IMPOSING, CORRUGATED RIDGES OF THE
KO'OLAU MOUNTAINS RISE ABOVE THE GREEN AND
YELLOW BANANA GROVES LINING THE NATURAL
AMPHITHEATERS BELOW.

THE NU'UANU PALI & THE WINDWARD BEACHES

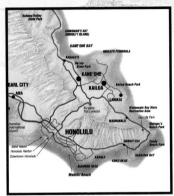

THIS RELATIVELY SHORT TOUR shows off O'ahu's most famous view and some of its best beaches. From Waikiki, follow the H-1 Freeway west to the Pali Highway exit. The Pali Highway climbs into cool Nu'uanu Valley, heading through the mountains to the Windward suburbs of Kailua and Kane'ohe.

First stop: A mile up the Pali Highway, look for signs on the right to Queen Emma's Summer Palace. The gracious, simple structure, set in a garden, serves as a small museum for memorabilia depicting the lifestyle of mid-nineteenth century Hawaiian royalty.

A mile beyond the palace, turn right onto Nu'uanu Pali Drive. This old road passes some of Honolulu's great old estates as it climbs the valley, finally leaving them behind in a tangle of

THE SUMMER PALACE OF QUEEN EMMA WAS USED AS A RETREAT AND SOCIAL CENTER UNTIL HER DEATH. TODAY THE DAUGHTERS OF HAWAI'I MAINTAIN IT AS A MUSEUM.

✱ ✱ ✱ ✱ ✱

rain forest. The Nu'uanu Pali drive rejoins the main Pali Highway. Another exit two miles later leads to one of the most famous views in Hawai'i: the Nu'uanu

Pali Lookout. From high above sheer cliffs (*pali*), Windward Oʻahu is spread out before you. The wind, funnelled up the cliffsides, can be treacherous, but mostly it's fun. The remains of the old, pre-tunnel Pali wagon road hug the cliff to the right of the lookout.

Return to the Pali Highway and head toward Kailua. Follow the Highway straight through to Kailua Beach Park. Famed for windsurfing, sparkling Kailua Bay's long, crescent beach is also a popular place for families, canoe paddlers, kayakers, and sun-worshippers, particularly early in the day. By late afternoon in normal trade wind weather, the sun is behind the clouds that pile up against the mountains.

Commercial ocean-sports companies use the beach park for windsurfing and kayaking lessons and it can get very busy. The quiet residential sections of the beach to the north can be reached via the beach-access paths along Kalaheo Avenue.

Lanikai, a lovely residential area, is a three-minute drive beyond Kailua Beach Park around Alala Point and offers one of Oʻahu's favorite (and least crowded) beaches noted for its calm, turquoise water and dazzling golden sand. Offshore are the picturesque twin Mokulua islands. To reach the beach, park along Mokulua Drive near one of the several beach rights-of-way between the million-dollar house lots.

Return to Honolulu and Waikiki by the same route, or circle the southeast corner of the island via Waimanalo and Makapuʻu Point into Honolulu.

KAILUA BEACH PARK PROVIDES PUBLIC ACCESS TO 30 ACRES OF ONE OF THE FINEST SWIMMING BEACHES AND THE BEST WINDSURFING AND CATAMARAN SAILING SPOTS.

A CHILD BOOGIEBOARDS THE WAVES AT THE BEACH FRONTING THE SMALL UPSCALE COMMUNITY OF LANIKAI.

ON THE WINDWARD SIDE, SUCH A MORNING LINE-UP OF CATAMARANS IS ABOUT AS CLOSE AS YOU'LL COME TO A TRAFFIC JAM.

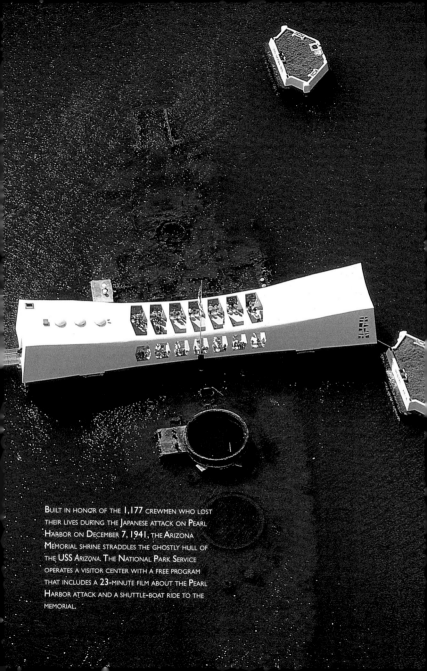

BUILT IN HONOR OF THE 1,177 CREWMEN WHO LOST
THEIR LIVES DURING THE JAPANESE ATTACK ON PEARL
HARBOR ON DECEMBER 7, 1941, THE ARIZONA
MEMORIAL SHRINE STRADDLES THE GHOSTLY HULL OF
THE USS ARIZONA. THE NATIONAL PARK SERVICE
OPERATES A VISITOR CENTER WITH A FREE PROGRAM
THAT INCLUDES A 23-MINUTE FILM ABOUT THE PEARL
HARBOR ATTACK AND A SHUTTLE-BOAT RIDE TO THE
MEMORIAL.

PEARL HARBOR & THE WAI'ANAE COAST

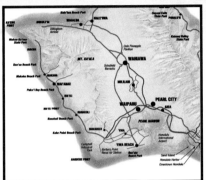

FROM WAIKIKI, TAKE THE H-1 Freeway west, carefully following signs past the airport to the USS *Arizona* Memorial exit, and the National Parks Service Visitor Center at the Pearl Harbor Naval Base. Reflecting its key role in America's entry in World War II, sprawling Pearl Harbor has been designated a National Historic Landmark, the only military base in the U.S. so recognized. Today, Pearl Harbor is as important as ever as the headquarters for the largest single military command in the world, CINCPAC (Commander-in-Chief of American Forces in the Pacific).

The Visitor Center offers a twenty-minute documentary film before visitors board the shuttle boat for a short trip to the USS *Arizona* Memorial. The film and Memorial boat ride are on a first-

RECENTLY RESTORED, THE "MIGHTY MO" IS OPEN 365 DAYS A YEAR FROM 9:00 AM TO 5:00 PM. LARGE VOLUNTEER GROUPS, INCLUDING VETERANS, REFURBISHED HER DECK, PAINT AND FITTINGS TO CREATE A LASTING MEMORIAL.

✳   ✳   ✳   ✳   ✳

come, first-served basis starting daily at 7:30 a.m. (except Monday). Waits can be very long.

The memorial itself is a simple, white-marble structure built over the submerged battleship that was sunk by Japanese torpedo bombs on December 7, 1941, with the loss of 1,100 Navy personnel. The names of the dead

IN 1965, A REPLICA OF THE OLD MAUI WHALING TOWN OF LAHAINA WAS RE-CREATED ON THIS SITE AT MAKUA BEACH FOR THE FILMING OF THE MOTION PICTURE *HAWAII*.

✳   ✳   ✳

are inscribed on one wall of the memorial. The ship was never decommissioned; her flag still flies, and rainbow-color oil slicks can be seen floating above the ship. Another attraction is the battleship USS *Missouri*, site of the Japanese surrender of World War II. Call 423-2263 for visitor information.

Leaving Pearl Harbor, take H-1 west to Wai'anae and the leeward coast, separated from the rest of the island by the Wai'anae mountain range. This most rural and "local" part of O'ahu is also the sunniest. Many parts of this area are Hawaiian homestead lands available to those of at least 50 percent Hawaiian ancestry under a 1922 act of the U.S. Congress. Wai'anae and its valley, once heavily populated, has a frontier feeling. But all along this coast, resort and golf developments, spurred by Japanese investments, have begun to alter the simple and easy-going Wai'anae lifestyle. The area now has some of the island's most effective grass-roots community organizations, committed to protecting local lifestyles and improving the educational and employment possibilities for their children.

As the H-1 Freeway bends around the southwest corner of the island and becomes Farrington Highway, you'll notice coconut palms and construction along the coast. This is Ko 'Olina (West Beach) and the location of the JW Marriott Ihilani Resort and Spa, where man-made beaches have been created from the rocky coast. Ambitious plans call for more hotels, luxury condo apartments, a marina, and several golf courses in the future. Nearby, on the vast 'Ewa plain, a consortium of private and public agencies are building the master-planned community called Kapolei, O'ahu's "second city."

North along Farrington Highway are the towns of Nanakuli, Ma'ili, Wai'anae, and Makaha, as well as Ma'ili Beach Park, Poka'i Bay Beach Park, Makua Beach Park. and Yokohama Beach at the far north end of the Highway. Like the North Shore, Wai'anae's beaches require caution during winter

THE KO ʻOLINA RESORT complex
IS A COMMUNITY OF LUXURY
RESIDENCES AND HOTELS BEING
BUILT AROUND CRESCENT-SHAPED
BEACHES NEAR BARBERS POINT.

THE BROAD SPLASHES OF SUNSET HUES PAINT THE EVENING SKY OFF MAʻILI POINT.

when big waves and strong currents can make swimming risky. In summer, the waters are generally harmless.

The deep, calm offshore waters are rich fishing and diving grounds. Wai'anae Boat Harbor, just beyond Poka'i Bay Beach Park, is home to many deep-sea-fishing charter boats and commercial diving operations.

Inland from Makaha is the restored Kane'aki Heiau. Once a scene of human sacrifices, the heiau is now one of the most completely restored Hawaiian temples in the state.

North of Makaha is gorgeous Makua Valley. Beyond is Kaneana Cave, the legendary home of the shark god's son. You can't miss it. At Yokohama the road ends and the trail to Ka'ena Point begins.

RESIDENTS OF THE WAI'ANAE COAST BELIEVE THAT THIS "IS THE CLOSEST THING TO AN UNSPOILED HAWAIIAN PLACE ON THIS ISLAND."

THIS BEAUTIFUL HARBOR AT POKA'I IS HOME TO FISHING AND PLEASURE BOATS ON THE WEST O'AHU COAST. LITERALLY TRANSLATED, POKA'I MEANS NIGHT OF THE SUPREME ONE."

MAUNA LAHILAHI OR "THIN MOUNTAIN" JUTS OUT INTO THE OCEAN FROM THE WHITE SANDS OF PAPAONEONE BEACH ON THE WAI'ANAE COAST.

THE DEEP WATER AND REEF NETWORK OFF THE WAI'ANAE COAST PROVIDE THE ENVIRONMENT FOR O'AHU'S MOST PROLIFIC FISHING GROUNDS.

LOOKING INTO THE HEART OF DOWNTOWN HONOLULU, UP BISHOP STREET FROM THE PARKING LOT FRONTING THE ALOHA TOWER MARKETPLACE.

DOWNTOWN HONOLULU

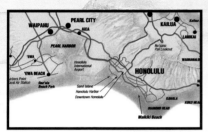

COMPLETED IN 1969 AT A COST OF $24.5 MILLION, THE
STATE CAPITOL BUILDING IS ALIVE WITH ACTIVITY FROM
FEBRUARY TO MAY, WHEN THE LEGISTLATURE IS IN SESSION.

❋ ❋ ❋ ❋ ❋

A WALKING TOUR OF Honolulu's compact and attractive downtown, easily accessible by a fifteen-minute bus ride from Waikiki hotels (parking is scarce and expensive), covers Hawai'i's corporate, banking, and government center located near many historical sites from early Honolulu.

Palm-lined Bishop Street is downtown's main north-south boulevard. Sleek high-rises and elegant, mission-style corporate headquarters create a unique architectural blend. Tanned businessmen in muted-print *aloha* shirts, and secretaries wearing *lei* and flowing *mu'umu'u* lend an unmistakably tropical feeling to one of America's most prosperous and exotic city centers. Narrow Merchant Street, which crosses Bishop Street two blocks from the waterfront, has vestiges amid the high rises of its nineteenth-century importance, including the extravagantly balustraded two-story Kamehameha IV post office building, and the tile-roofed, low-rise headquarters of *kama'aina* C. Brewer Company. The lobbies of the Amfac Building at the foot of Bishop Street and the Pau'ahi Tower on Bishop Square regularly host art exhibitions.

Two blocks *Diamond Head* along King Street is the civic center, Honolulu's handsomely landscaped collection of government buildings, including several of

Hawai'i's most historic landmarks. The one-time seat of the monarchy, 'Iolani Palace, was built in 1882 by King David Kalakaua after he returned from a grand tour of Europe. In the early years of statehood, the Palace served as the capitol until a new one was built nearby. Recently and impeccably restored, the Palace and its grounds, featuring broad lawns, a spreading banyan tree, and towering coconut groves, are the most pleasant spots in downtown Honolulu, especially at Friday lunchtime, when the Royal Hawaiian Band plays in the Victorian bandstand on the grounds. Tours of the Palace are available by appointment only.

WO FAT'S CHOP SUEY RESTAURANT, SERVING THE BEST CHINESE FOOD TO HONOLULU RESIDENTS SINCE 1882.

✳   ✳   ✳

The exuberant State Capitol Building, completed in 1969, is just *mauka* of the Palace. A statue of Queen Lili'uokalani, Hawai'i's last monarch (who was later imprisoned within the Palace by the businessmen who overthrew her regime), stands between the two buildings. Across from the Palace on King Street is Ali'iolani Hale, once the monarchy's parliament building and now the home of the State Supreme Court. It is the colonnaded backdrop for the famous statue of King Kamehameha I.

Royal history and missionary history converge at the New England-style Kawaiaha'o Church, built of coral stone in 1841. This Congregational church, dedicated to preaching the gospel in Hawaiian, hosted royal weddings, baptisms, and funerals. The small graveyard directly behind the church memorializes the New England mission-aries who played a central—and still controversial—role in Hawai'i's modern history. Many of the family names on the granite and marble markers still resonate in Hawai'i in corporation names, foundations, charitable trusts, street names, school buildings, and museum wings. The Mission Houses Museum next door features the oldest wood-frame house in Honolulu, shipped from New England and reassembled in 1821, and a very good gift shop with an excellent collection of Hawaiiana. Other historic buildings in the area include Washington Place, a nineteenth-century mansion once owned by Queen Liliu'okalani and now the official residence for Hawai'i's governor, and Honolulu Hale, the mission-style city hall on King Street opposite Kawaiaha'o Church.

Three blocks *'ewa* on the other side of Bishop Street is Chinatown, O'ahu's oldest intact urban neighborhood. Low-rise, nineteenth-century brick buildings house Chinese

THE KING KAMEHAMEHA STATUE, COMMISSIONED BY THE HAWAIIAN KINGDOM'S LEGISLATURE OF 1878 AND CAST IN PARIS IN 1880, BEARS LITTLE OR NO RESEMBLANCE TO KAMEHAMEHA THE GREAT. THE FIRST STATUE SANK OFF THE FALKLAND ISLANDS, BUT THE SECOND ARRIVED IN HONOLULU IN TIME FOR KING KALAUKAUA'S CORONATION IN 1883. IT NOW STANDS IN FRONT OF HAWAI'I'S OLD JUDICIARY BUILDING ON KING STREET.

'IOLANI PALACE, THE ONLY ROYAL PALACE IN THE UNITED STATES, RECENTLY UNDERWENT A NINE-YEAR RESTORATION THAT COST ALMOST $6 MILLION.

herbalists, flower shops, Vietnamese restaurants, raffish bars, X-rated theaters, chic art galleries, and dozens of eateries. Don't miss Wo Fat, a cacophonous Cantonese restaurant in a landmark Chinese-style building on Hotel Street, and the O'ahu Market, a pungent, open-air fish, produce, and flower market on the corner of King and Kekaulike Streets. Across Kekaulike Street is a Chinese market with a fascinating array of Chinese produce, spices, and flowers.

Across Nimitz Highway on the Honolulu waterfront, *Diamond Head* of the Aloha Tower, the Hawai'i Maritime Museum juts into the harbor. It offers an innovative and fascinating presentation of Hawai'i's economic and recreational ties to the ocean. This carefully thought-out, indoor-outdoor specialty museum is recommended for ocean-lovers of every stripe and every age. Alongside the museum, the century-old, Scottish-built, four-masted square-rigger, *Falls of Clyde*, tugs at her mooring lines.

THE ANCIENT "SHELTERED BAY" NAMED KOU BY THE HAWAIIANS OF OLD NOW SERVES HONOLULU AS THE PORT INTO THE LARGEST AND MOST IMPORTANT CITY IN THE CENTRAL PACIFIC. THE NEWLY RENOVATED ALOHA TOWER AND ITS UPSCALE MARKETPLACE SATISFY THE GROWING NEEDS OF THE REVITALIZED DOWNTOWN BUSINESS DITRICT.

THE VIEW OF DOWNTOWN HONOLULU FROM ACROSS THE HARBOR EXHIBITS ALL THE TRAPPINGS OF A MODERN METROPOLIS. THIS BUSINESS SECTOR OF THE CITY IS HOME TO MANY INTERNATIONAL CORPORATIONS.

THIS VIEW FROM AN UPPER FLOOR OF THE
SHERATON WAIKIKI LOOKS DOWN ON THE ROOF
OF THE PINK ROYAL HAWAIIAN HOTEL.
TOURMALINE BLUE WATERS, BRIGHTLY COLORED
CATAMARANS, AND THE FAMILIAR SILHOUETTE OF
DIAMOND HEAD IDENTIFY THIS STRETCH OF
TOWEL-COVERED SAND AS WAIKIKI BEACH, THE
JEWEL OF THE PACIFIC, THE MOST FAMOUS RESORT
AND RECREATION SPOT IN THE WORLD.

WAIKIKI

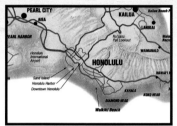

COCONUT-CUPPED TAHITIAN DANCERS TREAT GUESTS TO SPECTACULAR HULA DEMONSTRATIONS AT THE KODAK HULA SHOW.

❋   ❋   ❋   ❋

DIAMOND HEAD, THE MOST famous natural landmark on earth, provides a spectacular demarcation for the resort jewel of the Pacific: Waikiki. Blessed with white-sand beaches, varicolored sunsets, and warm tropical water, this lively haven welcomes visitors year round to bask in its playgrounds.

Numerous points of interest lie within walking distance from any hotel. A simple stroll down the beach toward Diamond Head, beginning at the Ala Wai yacht harbor at Waikiki's western edge, can provide valuable insight into the activities and adventures to be found in this resort paradise.

Every Friday afternoon, as the sun glides toward the horizon, boats parade out of the harbor in full sail. The Hawai'i Prince Hotel, with its amber-tinted windows, towers over the harbor and shines golden in the waning evening light. Walking down the beach toward Diamond Head, you pass the 'Ilikai Hotel, made famous by the opening montage of *Hawaii 5-0*. Next is the lagoon of the megalithic Hilton Hawaiian Village, with its multicolored catamaran rocking in the gentle shore break fronting the hotel. The Hale Koa, the military hotel, sits back on its property adjacent to Fort DeRussy, the official armed forces R & R post. The beach narrows at the Outrigger Reef Hotel and the prestigious Halekulani, with its *koa* wood paneling and orchid mosaic swimming pool. Here the stroll becomes an adventure along the seawall.

The gigantic Sheraton Waikiki complex casts a long afternoon shadow over the pink Royal Hawaiian Hotel. Lovingly called the "Pink Palace," this mission-style monument has graciously hosted discriminating guests since it opened on February 1, 1927.

A RAINBOW MOSAIC INSTANTLY IDENTIFIES THE OCEAN FRONT TOWER OF THE HILTON HAWAIIAN VILLAGE.

✳   ✳   ✳

The triplex of the Surfrider Hotel, with its two massive towers flanking the "Grande Dame" of Waikiki, the Moana Hotel, is the last collection of buildings at this end of the beach. Across Kalakaua Avenue are the Princess Ka'iulani, the Hyatt Regency Waikiki, Pacific Beach, and Hawaiian Regent hotels.

Kuhio Beach Park fronts Kalakaua in an open expanse of blue water. Vendors offer everything from surfboards for rent and outrigger canoe rides for hire, to surfing lessons, sodas, and sandwiches. There are lifeguards on duty, and a protected saltwater wading area for inexperienced swimmers.

Beyond this cluster of activity are the more subdued Gold Coast and Kapi'olani Park, local favorites for sunbathing and weekend gatherings. The park, rich in history, is named after Queen Kapi'olani, beloved wife of King Kalakaua. This green oasis in the shadow of Diamond Head was the scene of the first polo matches and horse races on O'ahu, and today is the end point for the Aloha Day and Kamehameha Day parades. Collected in the park are the Honolulu Zoo, the famous Waikiki Shell amphitheater where everyone from Fleetwood Mac to the New York Symphony has performed, the Kapi'olani Park Pavilion (home of the Kodak Hula Show presented Tuesdays, Wednesdays, and Thursdays at 10 am), public tennis courts, and a broad expanse of lawn where children and their parents congregate each weekend for AYSO (American Youth Soccer Organization) soccer, Pop Warner football, and little league baseball games.

Continuing toward Diamond Head, you'll find—across Kalakaua Avenue from Kapi'olani Park—Queen's Beach, a favorite sun spot for the gay community. The Natatorium, the largest salt-water pool in the U.S., was built in 1927 to honor the men and women of Hawai'i who fought in World War I. This relic of the past hosted swimming races in the days when Hawai'i's swimmers were frequent Olympians. Today it is closed to the public, pending restoration. Nearby, marine animals display their aquatic beauty at the Honolulu Aquarium.

THE GRAND MOANA HOTEL EXUDES THE GRACE AND ELEGANCE OF HER VICTORIAN PAST. HER TWIN TOWERS (FORMERLY THE TALLEST ON THE BEACH, BUT NOW DWARFED BY THEIR NEIGHBORS) STAND GUARD ON EITHER SIDE OF THE HOTEL'S FAMED BANYAN, CREATING A POCKET OF REGAL LEISURE.

HAWAIIAN ENTERTAINERS SERENADE DINNER GUESTS ON THE MANICURED BEACH FRONT LAWN OF THE HALEKULANI HOTEL, FAVORED BY VISITORS AND RESIDENTS ALIKE.

The area from Queen's Beach to the foot of Diamond Head is known as the Gold Coast. Condominiums, small hotels, exclusive clubs, and private homes line deserted beaches. The quaint cottages in this quiet, exclusive neighborhood harken back to a time when all of Waikiki was lulled by the hush of streets like these.

When visitors have had enough of the surf and sun, Waikiki offers a variety of landlubber's activities. At the Royal Hawaiian Shopping Center, the International Marketplace, and the Waikiki Shopping Plaza, visitors can purchase anything from custom-made knickknacks to designer clothing.

The Honolulu Zoo and the Honolulu Aquarium are wonderful stops for folks with children in tow, and the Kodak Hula Show at the Kapi'olani Park pavilion provides Hawaiian entertainment.

The Waikiki Trolley, an interesting-looking, San Francisco-style vehicle, makes regularly scheduled stops at the major hotels for pickups and will drop you at the front entrance of places like the Honolulu Art Academy, Bishop Museum, 'Iolani Palace, Kawaiaha'o Church, and the Mission Houses Museum. Take a camera; the ride is as good as the destination.

Dining is an adventure at the many ethnic restaurants in and around Waikiki. There are places offering Thai cuisine, Korean, Japanese, Mexican, Italian, French, Chinese, Hawaiian, and American fare. And, for the less hardy, there is a wide selection of standard fast-food outlets.

Waikiki prides itself on its ability to provide relaxation, sport, excitement, tranquillity, and luxury within its 500 acres. This is a wonderful place to people-watch. Stock up on lots of film, lots of sunscreen, and prepare yourself for the time of your life.

An outrigger canoe ride, one of the most inexpensive treats on Waikiki Beach, ranks near the top of the list of memory makers.

ABOVE: EACH WEEKEND KAPI'OLANI PARK FILLS WITH SOCCER-PLAYING CHILDREN, STUNT KITES, AND FAMILY GATHERINGS.

LEFT: PINK FLAMINGOS STRIKE EXOTIC POSES AT THEIR POOL JUST INSIDE THE ENTRANCE TO THE HONOLULU ZOO.

THE MODERN WAIKIKI TROLLEY HARKENS BACK TO A TIME WHEN THE ONLY TRANSPORTATION TO AND FROM WAIKIKI BEACH WAS THE TROLLEY, WITH MULE-DRAWN AND (LATER) ELECTRIC CARS. THIS REPLICA SAN FRANCISCO-STYLE TRAM USHERS VISITORS TO MANY POINTS OF INTEREST IN AND AROUND HONOLULU.

HONOLULU'S MUSEUMS & MEMORIALS

THE CITY'S MOST IMPORTANT cultural attractions are spread out beyond downtown Honolulu, and a car is the best way to reach them, although the city bus system will deliver you to each of them for less than a dollar. Reasonable entrance fees are the norm.

The Bishop Museum and Planetarium is the world's leading repository of Hawaiian and Polynesian cultural artifacts and natural history specimens, and is a very busy research facility. Its highly-polished *koa* wood exhibition halls showcase the history of Hawaii with ancient idols, feather capes, gourd implements, canoes, and a wealth of royal memorabilia. The Atherton Halau presents *hula* demonstrations at 1 p.m. every day.

The Honolulu Academy of Arts, with collections of Asian, European, and American art, is Hawai'i's largest museum. The handsome building is a hybrid of native, Oriental, and mission architectural styles dominated by a sweeping, double-hipped Hawaiian roof line that shelters cool interior courtyards. Across Beretania Street is Thomas Square, Honolulu's first planned park. The Academy is easily reachable by city bus from Waikiki to South Beretania Street at Ward Avenue in central Honolulu.

The Contemporary Museum, a jewel-like display of American, Asian, and local art, has recently taken up residence in a renovated, lovely Makiki mansion in the residential hills high above the city. The architecture of the 1925 house is a sophisticated blend of Japanese style and Hawaiian grace, all set into a rolling, shady garden with peek-a-boo views of the city and the sea. The small indoor-outdoor cafe is one of Honolulu's secret lunch spots.

✻   ✻   ✻   ✻   ✻

OPPPOSITE: PUNCHBOWL CRATER, ONCE KNOWN TO HAWAIIANS AS PUOWAINA, OR "THE HILL FOR PLACING (OF SACRIFICES)," IS TODAY FAMOUS AS THE LOCATION OF THE NATIONAL MEMORIAL CEMETERY OF THE PACIFIC, WHERE MORE THAN 21,000 SERVICEMEN, WHO SERVED IN WORLD WARS I AND II AND THE KOREAN AND VIETNAM WARS, ARE BURIED. THE VETERANS' GRAVES ARE MARKED BY SMALL WHITE CROSSES THAT GEOMETRICALLY COVER THE CRATER'S 112-ACRE FLOOR. EACH YEAR DURING MEMORIAL DAY CELEBRATIONS, THE INDIVIDUAL GRAVES ARE DECORATED. THE 26,280 FIGHTING MEN LISTED AS "MISSING IN ACTION" ARE COMMEMORATED IN A "COURTS OF THE MISSING" MONUMENT ON PUNCHBOWL'S INTERIOR 'EWA SLOPE.

THE BISHOP MUSEUM'S KOA-PANELED GREAT HALL HOUSES GLASS CASES FILLED WITH CARVED AND FEATHER GODS, CAPES, AND OTHER REMNANTS OF PRE-CONTACT HAWAI'I.

✵   ✵   ✵

Also best by car—or tour bus since parking may be difficult—is the **National Memorial Cemetery of the Pacific,** better known as Punchbowl. This low volcanic cone rises directly behind downtown Honolulu. Within its shallow crater are the final resting places of thousands of America's war dead, and 28,000 more who never returned home are memorialized on the marble walls of the Courts of the Missing. Impressive murals chart the course of war in the Pacific, from World War II to Vietnam. Over five million people visit Punchbowl every year to relive some of America's most wrenching battles and to remember its heroes.

MRS. CHARLES MONTAGUE COOKE ENVISIONED, BUILT, AND ENDOWED THE HONOLULU ART ACADEMY OF ARTS IN 1927.

THE TERRACED COURTYARD OF THE CONTEMPORARY MUSEUM ABOVE DOWNTOWN HONOLULU
IS THE OUTDOOR DISPLAY AREA FOR AVANT-GARDE ORIENTAL, EUROPEAN, AND AMERICAN ART.

High above Niu Valley on O'ahu's south shore, the upper class security-gate subdivision of Hawai'i Loa Ridge features luxury mansions huddled together in tight clusters, with pools close enough to tempt one to jump from one tiled swimming hole into another.

HONOLULU'S NEIGHBORHOODS

EITHER BY THE BUS or car, with a good map, wander around the neighborhoods to learn something about Hawai'i's complex social fabric. It's the Honolulu most visitors never see.

The city is a patchwork of neighborhoods, some defined by valleys and ridges, others by economic or old-time ethnic distinctions. Low-rise Kaimuki and high-rise Moili'ili, close to Waikiki, have been middle-class Japanese strongholds since those neighborhoods were first laid out in the 1920s. Kaimuki, particularly its main thoroughfare, Wai'alae Avenue, with its small shops, diners, and "crack-seed" stores, has a pre-World War II feel. The residential side streets reveal simple houses, with neat, well-tended plots, and an enviable domestic pride.

The Moili'ili business district along King Street at University Avenue serves local residents and the nearby University of Hawai'i community. Flower stalls, small medical offices, and *saimin* stands share the sidewalks with copy shops, pizza parlors, book shops and a variety of health-food stores and ethnic restaurants.

Manoa, the large, deep valley behind the University of Hawai'i, directly *mauka* of Waikiki, is interesting for its fine, pre-World War II homes, built when neighborhoods were clearly separated along racial lines. The misty rains of Manoa are responsible for frequent afternoon rainbows, thus the University of Hawai'i's athletic teams are the Rainbows—or, simply, the "Bows."

A BROAD ASSORTMENT OF CHINESE DESSERTS IN CHINATOWN—DRIED FRUITS COOKIES, ALMOND COOKIES, AND SWEET PASTRIES.

Manoa and the other valleys behind Honolulu (Palolo, Pauoa, Nuʻuanu, and Kalihi) emit the sense of modesty and contentment typical of post-World War II middle-class life in Honolulu.

Separating the valleys is a series of broad, high ridges, dense with single-family homes. At night, the lights of St. Louis Heights and Maunalani Heights, when viewed from Kapiʻolani Park or the Ala Wai Canal in Waikiki, seem to float in the blackness. Long ago a poet labeled them "stairways to heaven." These neighborhoods, where real-estate prices rise faster than the elevation, have some of Honolulu's finest views, day or night.

THE 2,013-FOOT RIDGE OF PUʻU ʻOHIʻA, "HILL OF THE ʻOHIA" TREES, WAS RENAMED BY THIRSTY HIKERS IN HONOR OF THE GREEK KING TANTALUS

✻   ✻   ✻

Honolulu's *haole* aristocrats initially set up housekeeping in cool Nuʻuanu Valley, on the Makiki and Tantalus heights, and later on the seaward slopes of Diamond Head where Noela Drive and Diamond Head Road still display Honolulu's grand, oligarchical past.

Kahala and Waiʻalae, east of Diamond Head, are newer, once predominantly *haole* neighbor-hoods—built on old pig farms and duckponds after World War II. The tacit segregation died in the 1960s, and local prosperity —plus investors from the Far East—has produced a cosmopolitan mix in these suburbs.

Kalihi, ʻewa of downtown, is full of Hawaiʻi's most recent immigrants and some of its oldest old-timers. Often raffish and down-at-the-heels, Kalihi just looks quaint, especially along North King Street, which has a definite pre-World War II feeling. Filipinos, Vietnamese, Cambodians, Koreans, and Samoans, as well as third-generation Japanese and native Hawaiians, share the turf in Kalihi, at the same time providing some of the best—and cheapest—ethnic food in Honolulu. This book is not meant to be a dining guide, but an exception must be made for **Helena's Hawaiian Food** in Kalihi. This modest restaurant, opened in 1945, is a cultural prize for any visitor. The food is authentic Hawaiian and tasty, and the warmth of the place is truly a revelation.

THE PRESTIGIOUS COMMUNITY OF BLACK POINT IS THE LOCATION OF DORIS DUKE'S SHANGRI-LA MANSION.

Lanikai Beach

Located between Kailua Bay and Waimanalo Bay, the mile-long stretch of calm water known as Lanikai beach was once an ancient fishing spot. Developers misunderstood Hawaiian in naming it; Lanikai literally translated means "sea heaven," not "heavenly sea." Two offshore islands called the Mokuluas are protected bird sanctuaries.

BEACHES

O'AHU'S 112 MILES OF shoreline have at least one beach to satisfy every taste: the very sunny, calm—and crowded—waters and sand spas of the South Shore; peaceful lagoons and lush, tropical Windward strands; raging winter surf and summer snorkeling on the North Shore; and the arid Wai'anae coast's continuous stretch of sand, surf, and sunsets.

Beach culture thrives on O'ahu. Honolulu's urbanites hit the beaches at all hours for morning, lunchtime, and after-work swims. On weekends, O'ahu's sandy fringe is thick with *hibachis*, volleyball games, and all-day picnicking families and overnight campers. A survey confirmed what many had long suspected: residents drive farther to work than to their recreation.

Acknowledged as the most reliable surf spots on earth, O'ahu's beaches are laboratories for the latest radical wave maneuvers and the latest radical surf fashions. Surf culture around the world takes its cues from Ala Moana, Sandy Beach, and the North Shore. New York, Los Angeles, and Tokyo recognize the potency of O'ahu's youth-oriented surf scene and use images of its high-energy beaches and bronzed bodies to sell everything from dry beer to cars, sunglasses, soda, chewing gum, and waterproof lipstick.

Sixty-three beach parks dot O'ahu's coastline. Some do not have lifeguards on duty regularly. Most have restrooms, shower facilities, and parking. Most are visible from the coastal highway. Popular Waimanalo and Bellows Beach are hidden from Kalaniana'ole Highway by woods. At Kahala, Kailua, Lanikai, La'ie,

Malaekahana, and Sunset, beach-front homes mask much of the shore.

Note: All beaches in Hawai'i are public up to the vegetation line above the high-water mark. Even in exclusive residential areas and at beachside resorts, public access to the shore must be provided. Beach rights-of-way from public roads are marked—some better than others.

The following "menu" lists O'ahu's best-known, best-loved, and often best-kept-secret beaches, and is designed to help you program your perfect beach day. Spend at least one complete day at a beach, preferably one facing west to the sunset. Take plenty of food and water, a beach umbrella, sun block, swim fins and snorkeling gear. Don't forget books, a shirt and long pants (right after sunset you'll feel chilled if you've been getting sun most of the day).

WAIMANALO BEACH / BELLOWS BEACH

THIS UNCROWDED FIVE-MILE STRETCH OF FINE SAND AND TURQUOISE WATER IS A LOCAL FAVORITE FOR FAMILIES AND SOLITARY BOOK READERS. THE VIEWS OF OUTLYING ISLANDS AND THE WAIMANALO CLIFFS ARE STUNNING. THE WIDE, SANDY BEACH. GENTLY SLOPING OCEAN BOTTOM, AND SMALL WAVES ARE PERFECT FOR FAMILY FUN. THE SHORELINE FALLS UNDER TWO JURISDICTIONS, EACH WITH DIFFERENT RULES: WAIMANALO BEACH PARK IS RUN BY THE CITY, AS IS WAIMANALO BAY RECREATION CENTER, WHICH PERMITS CAMPING; AND BELLOWS AIR FORCE STATION, WHICH OPENS ITS BEACH ONLY ON WEEKENDS. ALL THREE AREAS OFFER PARKING, BUT CAR BREAK-INS ARE A PROBLEM HERE.

ALA MOANA BEACH PARK

URBAN HONOLULU'S BIGGEST AND BEST BEACH ATTRACTS CROWDS TO ITS GENTLE WATERS AND BROAD LAWNS, ESPECIALLY ON WEEKENDS, WHEN HUGE FAMILY PICNICS AND SPORTS ACTIVITIES GIVE A FESTIVE ATMOSPHERE TO THE 76-ACRE PARK. THE WIDE REEF-PROTECTED BEACH HAS EXCELLENT SWIMMING, WITH A DEEP CHANNEL 20 YARDS OFFSHORE FOR LONG-DISTANCE SWIMMERS TO PRACTICE. PADDLING TEAMS LAUNCH THEIR OUTRIGGER CANOES FROM THE 'EWA END OF THE BEACH. AT THE DIAMOND HEAD END, MAN-MADE MAGIC ISLAND PENINSULA OFFERS A PROTECTED SWIMMING COVE WITH STUNNING VIEWS OF DIAMOND HEAD, HONOLULU, AND THE SURF SITES ON THE OUTSIDE REEF. ALA MOANA BEACH PARK FRONTS THE ALA MOANA SHOPPING CENTER, 'EWA OF WAIKIKI, AND THE ALA WAI BOAT HARBOR ON ALA MOANA BOULEVARD. THERE ARE LIFEGUARDS, PARKING, RESTROOMS, FOOD CONCESSIONS, TENNIS COURTS, AND ATHLETIC FIELDS.

WAIKIKI BEACH

The world's most famous beach has a history to match its glamor. Waikiki has been a recreational refuge ever since Polynesians first settled on O'ahu. In the nineteenth century, Hawaiian royalty built wooden cottages here to escape dusty Victorian Honolulu, to relax among the broad lawns and cool breezes and to surf, fish, and "surf-bathe." Today's Royal Hawaiian Hotel, the gracious "Pink Palace," occupies the site of the ancient compound called Helumoa; and some of its tall palms are survivors from the Helumoa royal groves.

Makapu'u

LIKE ITS NEIGHBOR SANDY BEACH, MAKAPU'U IS A MECCA FOR
EXPERT BODY-BOARDERS AND BODYSURFERS -- BUT IT DEMANDS
CAUTION FROM EVERYBODY ELSE. NEVERTHELESS, THIS EXCEPTIONALLY
BEAUTIFUL BEACH, IN A COVE AT THE BASE OF MASSIVE MAKAPU'U
HEAD, IS POPULAR WITH ALL BEACHGOERS. THE WATERS CLOSE TO
SHORE ARE SAFER THAN THOSE AT SANDY BEACH AND ON CALM
DAYS OFFER A GOOD CHANCE TO FROLIC IN THE SURF AND LEARN
THE BASICS OF BODYSURFING. CONSULT THE LIFEGUADS BEFORE
ENTERING -- AND WEAR FINS. THE SCENERY HERE IS ENHANCED BY
TWO OFFSHORE BIRD SANCTUARIES: MANANA (RABBIT) AND
KAOHIKAIPU ISLANDS. BEST TIME OF DAY: MORNING THROUGH EARLY
AFTERNOON. AFTER 4 P.M., THE SUN SINKS BEHIND THE WAIMANALO
PALI AND ONSHORE BREEZES COOL THE BEACH CONSIDERABLY.

Ka'alawai Beach

SET AT THE BASE OF DIAMOND HEAD WHERE BLACK
POINT JUTS ONTO THE SEA, KA'ALAWAI IS A
PICTURESQUE SPOT FOR PASSIVE BEACH-GOING: TANNING,
READING, AND SWIMMING IN RELATIVE SOLITUDE. THE
PALM-FRINGED BEACH FRONTS BEAUTIFUL HOMES AND
OFFERS GREAT SPECTATOR VIEWS OF WAVE-JUMPING
WINDSURFERS WORKING THE TRADE WINDS. A SHORT,
ROCKY WALK OUT ALONG BLACK POINT LEADS TO AN
UNUSUAL SWIMMING AREA CALLED "DUKE'S," SO NAMED
BECAUSE IT WAS ONCE THE PRIVATE BOAT HARBOR FOR
HEIRESS DORIS DUKE'S HOME ON THE HILL ABOVE.

SANDY BEACH

One of O'ahu's favorite surfing spots, Sandy Beach is to some a way of life. The beach itself is a short, wide stretch of sand at the base of Koko Crater, facing the windy, turbulent Kaiwi Channel and the distant islands of Moloka'i and Lana'i. Trade wind-propelled waves hit the unprotected beach with maximum force, creating a dangerous shorebreak. Only O'ahu's experienced body-boarders and body-surfers revel in the steep "drops" and glassy "tubes." It only looks easy—it's not. The waves break in almost no water and are life-threatning to the inexperienced. The beach is repeatedly put off-limits to military personnel after too many drownings. There are daily rescues, as well as frequent neck and back injuries. Newcomers should check with the lifeguards before entering the water. If you do decide to "chance 'em," wear fins.

KAILUA BEACH

A FEW YEARS AGO, THIS BROAD, THREE-MILE STRETCH ALONG
BREEZY KAILUA BAY ON THE WINDWARD SIDE WAS THE
WINDSURFING CAPITAL OF THE WORLD. WINDSURFERS ARE STILL
AROUND, BUT THE HEAVY ACTION HAS MOVED TO DIAMOND
HEAD REEF AND TO THE NORTH SHORE OF MAUI. KAILUA
BEACH PARK, AT THE SOUTH END OF THE BEACH, IS BUSY ON THE
WEEKENDS, BUT THE MANY PUBLIC-ACCESS ALLEYS ALONG
RESIDENTIAL KALAHEO AVENUE PROVIDE PLENTY OF VIRTUALLY
DESERTED BEACHFRONT TO CHOOSE FROM. THE WATER COLORS
HERE ARE DAZZLING, AS IS THE QUALITY OF THE GOLDEN SAND.
WAVES BREAKING CLOSE TO SHORE, PARTICULARLY IN THE
MIDDLE SECTION OF THE BEACH, ARE GREAT FOR BEGINNING
BODYSURFERS AND BODY-BOARDERS.

DURING THE WINTER MONTHS FROM OCTOBER
THROUGH APRIL, THE NORTH SHORE BOOMS WITH THE
SOUNDS OF 10- TO 30-FOOT BREAKERS THAT WALL UP
AND CREST IN SPECTACULAR DISPLAYS OF POWER.
SURFERS FROM ALL OVER THE WORLD FLOCK TO THE
SHORES AND PLUNGE INTO THE SWELLS TO TEST THEIR
COURAGE AGAINST NATURE'S MOST BEAUTIFUL
CREATIONS.

ADVENTURES

LEADING OFF WITH THE ancient sports of surfing and outrigger-canoe racing, Hawai'i's high-energy wind and sea conditions have made it the water-sports capital of the world. International athletes flock here for surf contests, long-distance swimming races, deep sea fishing tournaments, inter-island canoe and kayak races, windsurfing contests, and trans-Pacific yacht races. On shore, brawny triathletes, daring hang-gliders, and mud-stained hikers carry the "just do it" ethos to new extremes. There is energy everywhere in Hawai'i: in the big mid-Pacific water, in the stiff winds, and on these young volcanic islands themselves.

Kayaking

Ocean kayaks, or surf skis, arrived from Australia about ten years ago. Local paddlers refined and lightened the craft for Hawaiian waters and now the sport is booming. For many, ocean kayak "runs" have replaced jogging as the regular exercise of choice.

Novices to this brawny sport find it pretty tricky, and an introductory lesson or two is recommended. After that, the ultralight, eighteen-foot fiberglass boats knife through the water with exhilarating speed. Kayaking's muscle-building and

THESE SURFBOARDS ARE AVAILABLE FOR RENT ON THE BEACH AT WAIKIKI.

cardiovascular benefits are unsurpassed, and the sport is a great way to get out on the water.

O'ahu hosts a regular series of long-distance ocean kayak races in the spring, culminating in the thirty-two-mile Kanaka Ikaika race across the wild Kaiwi Channel between Moloka'i and O'ahu in May.

SPINNAKER SAILING OFF WAIKIKI IS A PARTY ON WATER.

✳   ✳   ✳

For more water-fun adventure, look for tour companies offering fully-provisioned kayaking trips along the Windward coast of O'ahu, and expeditions along the spectacular north shore of Moloka'i during summer (highly recommended).

On the Waikiki side of O'ahu, **Go Bananas** rents and sells both "hard-shell" and inflatable kayaks and other water equipment, and can advise on water sports in general.

Walking and Hiking

Nothing gives a more intimate sense of place than a long walk. On O'ahu, three recommended hikes of moderate difficulty will give you some memorable encounters with O'ahu's diverse landscapes.

Diamond Head: The jaunt to Diamond Head's 763-foot summit shows off the landmark's interior crater, its maze of military fortifications (dug into the slopes during World War II) and, once on top, picture-perfect southern O'ahu and the Pacific. In ancient times, the Hawaiians lit bonfires on the summit to guide fishing canoes home. Diamond Head's actual name, "Le'ahi," means "the brow of the tuna." British sailors renamed the old volcano when they found bits of volcanic glass at its base and thought they were diamonds.

To reach the trail, enter the crater via the marked road off Monsarrat Avenue. Parking and the trail head are clearly marked. Bring water, your camera, and a flashlight for exploring the eerie tunnels and underground bunkers.

Ka'ena Point: Hawaiians believed that when a person was on his deathbed, his soul would leave his body to fulfill remaining earthly obligations, then travel to Ka'ena, the northwestern most point of O'ahu to depart the physical world.

Unearthly Ka'ena Point is accessible only to hikers, by a three-mile walk along the undeveloped coast. Aside from the distance, the route is not difficult, and the scenic and spiritual rewards are profound. The shoreline is edged by lava cliffs and boulders. The only places for swimming are a few rocky pools at the point, safe only when the normally turbulent sea is calm. In

Traditional canoe paddling teams practice regularly on the Ala Wai Canal for island-wide, state-wide and international competitions.

For a small fee, a pair of Waikiki beachboys will take you on the canoe ride of your life.

winter, the same ocean swells that make the North Shore famous give Ka'ena Point the largest breaking waves in all Hawai'i.

Ka'ena Point State Preserve is accessible on foot from the north end of Farrington Highway on the Wai'anae coast (about three miles), or from the western end of Farrington Highway on the North Shore (also about three miles). At either highway dead-end,

O'AHU'S MANY BEACHES PROVIDE THE IDEAL, FLAT SPACE NEEDED TO LAUNCH AN OUTRIGGER CANOE.

✻   ✻   ✻

parking areas mark the beginning of the trail. *Warning: do not leave valuables in your car.*

Sailing

Sailing is the sport of going nowhere slowly and at great expense. A sailboat is a hole in the water into which you pour your children's inheritance.

All true, but with a stiff trade wind just abaft the starboard beam, a high tropical island on the horizon, and some good music issuing from the waterproof boom-box, sailing is pure romance.

Hawai'i's sailing is somewhat circumscribed by the rough channels between the islands. Still, the southwestern leeward waters offer some great sailing and breathtaking perspectives. From a sailboat you'll gain

new appreciation of how isolated and in-significant these mid-ocean islands really are. The deep water is indescribably blue. During the sail you may see porpoises, flying fishes, or sea turtles, and, in late winter-early spring, vacationing whales from the Bering Sea. After a few hours you begin to understand how the early explorers, whalers, and adventurers felt when, after months on the open ocean, they gazed on these mysterious, legendary islands.

Be sure to check out sailing charter outfits that offer half-day, full-day and customized long-distance cruises out of both Honolulu and Kane'ohe. Outings can be tailored for snorkeling, sunset dinner sails, wedding cruises, overnight trips to the Wai'anae coast and longer trips to the Neighbor Islands.

Windsurfing

Hawai'i is a windsurfer's mecca. The wind and sea conditions are perfect for the sport; in fact, most advances in windsurfing design and technique develop in Hawai'i. From flat-water speed runs at Ma'alaea Bay on Maui to the radical wave-launched flips and loops

A SUNSET SAIL IN THE CALM WAVES OFF WAIKIKI BEACH IS AN UNFORGETTABLE ROMANTIC EXPERIENCE.

TOUR COMPANIES OFFER DAY TRIPS INTO THE AZURE WATERS OFF WAIKIKI FOR SAILING AND SNORKELING. EACH TOUR INCLUDES A CATERED GOURMET LUNCH.

A FLOATING GARDEN OF WIND-BLOSSOMED SAILS
GLIDES THROUGH THE ALA WAI YACHT HARBOR
CHANNEL TOWARD THE OPEN SEA.

at Diamond Head, it's all here. Of course, most of us will never have the pleasure of landing a windsurfer rig after a twenty-foot vault, nor will we soon be doing wind-dances on the face of fifteen-foot waves. Nevertheless, the uniquely exhilarating com-bination of wind, water, and muscle make this young sport very popular even in its more pedestrian forms.

Learning the basics of windsurfing can be arduous and frustrating. Plan on spending a few back-breaking learning hours in the water. Lessons are worth it for first-timers.

LOCAL SURFERS ALSO ENJOY THE WATERS OF WAIKIKI WHICH OFFER LONG, CALM RIDES.

✳   ✳   ✳

The best place on O'ahu to brush up your technique is at Kailua Beach. The winds are onshore, so you won't wind up in Tahiti, and there are usually enough other novices so you won't give up from embarrassment. Windsurfing rental and instruction outfits operate from Kailua Beach.

Scuba and Snorkeling

Most of O'ahu's best dive sites are off the Wai'anae coast, where light winds and minimal rainfall keep the water calm and clear. The most popular dive is on the swim-through wreck of the old Navy minesweeper *Mahi* in ninety feet of water. Nearby at seventy feet is a sunken Beechcraft cargo plane called, simply, "the plane." Also nearby are the Makaha Caves and the Land of Oz in fifty feet of water. These are lava formations—caves, tubes, arches and ledges—full of marine life.

Snorkelers head for Hanauma Bay (see Beaches), the North Shore during the summer, and all along the Wai'anae coast. Pupukea Beach Park on the North Shore has two popular, summer-only snorkeling and dive sites—Shark's Cove and Three Tables. They have generally clear water and plenty of fish.

Numerous dive shops offer introductory, all-inclusive boat dives, PADI-certified, two-tank boat dives (day and night), and certification classes. **Destination Hawai'i**, phone (808) 538-6200, is the clearinghouse for diving and scuba information. Contact them for a comprehensive twenty-four-page guide book.

Natural Outings

For those who find windsurfing or diving the reefs a little too radical, here are a few low-key ways to experience O'ahu's beauty.

The **Foster Botanical Garden** and the **Lyon Arboretum** are Honolulu's outstanding gardens, known for their collections of mature palms, exotic trees, and endemic Hawaiian species. The twenty-acre

KIDS OF ALL AGES CAN
AMUSE THEMSELVES FOR
HOURS IN THE WATER
WONDERLAND JUST
OUTSIDE MAJOR HOTELS.

READING IN THE SHADE, OR TANNING IN THE SUN, OR STROLLING ON THE SAND—ALL ARE A PLEASURE WITH WAIKIKI'S
PERFECT WEATHER.

LUCKY DIVERS AND SNORKELERS CAN SPOT THE LARGE
HAWAIIAN TURTLES, *HONU*, SWIMMING WITH SLOW GRACE
OVER REEFS NOT FAR FROM SHORE. THESE GENTLE SEA
CREATURES WERE ONCE HUNTED ALMOST TO EXTINCTION
BUT ARE NOW MAKING A GRADUAL COMEBACK.

Foster Garden, close to downtown, is open daily.

The 124-acre Lyon Arboretum, deep in Manoa Valley, is a working University of Hawai'i research facility, open to the public on the first Friday, the third Wednesday, and the third Saturday of each month. Reservations are recommended for the Arboretum's informative tours.

Guided tours of historic **Moanalua Valley and Gardens** just west of Honolulu are a chance to learn about the Hawaiians who once thrived in this valley and left behind archaeological evidence, including petroglyphs and stone terraces where *taro* was cultivated. Guides narrate the fascinating history of the valley and demonstrate how the Hawaiians used the plants growing along the route for rope, sandals, and building materials. The gardens are notable for their massive, spreading monkeypod trees.

Guided walking tours of the valley are offered by the Moanalua Gardens Foundation. Call ahead for more information; bring your lunch and some money for a donation.

TAKE A QUIET, LEISURELY WALK THROUGH FOSTER BOTANICAL GARDEN TO LEARN MORE ABOUT THE INDIGENOUS AND INTRODUCED FLORA AND FAUNA THAT CAN BE FOUND THROUGHOUT THE ISLAND.

THE SOFT SHADOWS OF EVENING SPREAD OVER THE SANDS
AND ACROSS THE WATER AS THE PLEASURES OF NIGHT LIFE
TAKE OVER.

CIVILIZATION

FROM DELUXE OCEAN-VIEW hotel dining rooms to fast-food on every corner, from dress shops that compete with Fifth Avenue to Hong Kong-style trinket booths, there's plenty in Waikiki to divert you from the beach.

Shopping

Beyond the tourist shops and designer boutiques of Waikiki lies a world of shopping for unique gifts, clothes and souvenirs. Your first destination should be **Ala Moana Center**, even if you don't like to shop. Within walking distance of Waikiki hotels and easily reached by bus, this 180-store behemoth is a total sensory experience. The bustling, ever-changing mall is advertised as "Hawai'i's Center," and it is. Everyone comes here because everything is here…everything.

Three other shopping (and dining) magnets, a little more "boutique-y" and diverse, are **Ward Centre** and **Ward Warehouse**, twin urban malls on Ala Moana Boulevard, between Waikiki and downtown; and upscale **Kahala Mall** in suburban Kahala.

A few city districts are worth checking out, too: **Kapahulu Avenue** with antique and collectibles stores and small crafts shops; **Chinatown** for art and

WYLAND GALLERY IN HALE'IWA IS ONE OF SEVERAL GALLERIES AROUND THE ISLAND OF O'AHU THAT OFFER SEASCAPE OILS AND SCULPTURES TO WELL-HEELED VISITORS AND RESIDENTS.

crafts, galleries and exotic Chinese apothecaries and gift stores; and **Waikele** in Kapolei for outlets galore.

For the best in Hawaiiana and Pacific books, crafts, and art prints, the **Shop Pacifica** at Bishop Museum; the **Mission Houses Gift Shop** at the Mission Houses Museum downtown; and the **Academy Shop** at the Honolulu Academy of Arts are recommended.

THE LIGHTS OF HONOLULU SPARKLE AGAINST THE BACKDROP OF SUNSET COLORS.

✳   ✳   ✳

For a fine selection of native Hawaiian crafts, try the **Little Hawaiian Craft Shop** in the Royal Hawaiian Shopping Center in Waikiki. The **Hula Supply Center** on King Street in Mo'ili'ili has been selling *hula* equipment, including gourds, bamboo nose flutes, *pahu* drums, raffia skirts, '*uli-'uli* (feathered gourds), Hawaiian and Tahitian print fabrics, etc., for years. Browsing here should give you some ideas about unique and au-thentic Hawaiian souvenirs and gifts. The best fresh flower *lei* **stands** are along Mauna-kea Street in Chinatown and on King Street in Mo'ili'ili. *Lei* here are less expensive than at the airport or in Waikiki, and usually better and fresher. Most florists will ship flowers for you.

For the latest surf-inspired clothing and gear, **Local Motion** in Waikiki, is tops.

Splash in the Ala Moana Center sells a mind-boggling assortment of women's swimwear from the briefest to more modest apparel.

Dining

The best-known Waikiki restaurants are the deluxe hotel dining rooms. Be prepared to dress and to open your pocketbook, but you can be assured of world-class dining.

Elsewhere in Waikiki, the food ranges from gourmet to familiar fast-food outlets.

Other busy dining centers have grown up along Ala Moana Boulevard, 'ewa of Waikiki: **Ward Centre, Aloha Tower, and Restaurant Row.** These three malls attract well-dressed local folks to their upscale restaurants and trendy bistros.

For the rest of Honolulu, restaurants are geared to a local clientele. One of the most popular spots for regional Hawaiian cuisine is **Sam Choy's Restaurant** on Kapahulu Avenue. Internationally-renowned chef Sam Choy has prepared a menu of exotically flavored entrees that has become a trademark for this comfortable dining venue. Call ahead for reservations: the food is so "*ono*" that seating is at a premium every day of the week.

HAWAIIAN CULTURAL LIFE IS RICH IN PAGEANTRY THAT CELEBRATES THE PAST GLORIES OF CHIEFS AND KINGS.

NO *HULA* ENSEMBLE IS COMPLETE WITHOUT ITS COLORFULLY-DRESSED SINGERS AND MUSICIANS, OFTEN ALL FAMILY MEMBERS.

Because of Honolulu's cosmopolitan makeup, ethnic food reigns—even the busiest fast-food places are essentially ethnic restaurants serving "plate lunch" and *saimin*.

Thai restaurants continue to be popular, particularly a string **(Keo's, Mekong I & II)** run by the Sananikone family. Italian restaurants include **Auntie Pasta's and Verbano**, among others. Japanese restaurants, *sushi* bars, and *yakiniku* shops are everywhere, including **Yanagi Sushi** on Kapiolani Boulevard; as are Chinese *dim-sum*, Cantonese, and Szechuan restaurants: **Yong Sing, China House,** and **Woodlands.** For the best Hawaiian food, try **Helena's Hawaiian Food** on North King Street in Kalihi, or **Ono's Hawaiian Food** on Kapahulu Avenue near Waikiki.

Nightlife

Waikiki is one of the centers of Honolulu's nightlife, which you'll quickly realize when you step onto its traffic-choked boulevards any Friday or Saturday night. It's all there: the bars, clubs, discos, and movie theaters. Most clubs are open until 2 a.m., some until 4 a.m.

Among the world's best watering holes are the beachfront bars along Waikiki Beach, where the sheer romance of a sunset or moonlight cock-tail can be over-whelming.

Outside of Waikiki are the major nightlife scenes at Restaurant Row and

THE NOSTALGIA OF "BOAT DAY" IS RECREATED, WHEN *HULA* DANCERS ONCE WELCOMED GLAMOUROUS LUXURY LINERS THAT DOCKED ALONGSIDE THE ALOHA TOWER.

the Aloha Tower complex. Here is an alternative array of pubs, cabarets, nightclubs, and discos.

The masters of Hawaiian music can usually be found playing somewhere in Waikiki or Honolulu, including at community fundraisers and charity events: **The Brothers Cazimero, The Peter Moon Band, Haunani Apoliona, Genoa Keawe, Frank Hewitt, Jerry Santos, Theresa Bright, Puamana, The Makaha Sons of Ni'ihau, Butch Helemano,** the **Pandanus Club, Marlene Sai, Cecilio and Kapono,** and **The Lim Family**. Watch for them.

Be on the lookout, also, for local comedian **Frank De Lima**, the beloved "Portagee" clown prince. He is usually causing trouble in some hotel showroom during any given week. He exploits the islands' racial pieties and local/tourist tensions for some great laughs. If you're in the front row, be prepared.

Waikiki at night casts its unique spell, beckoning visitors to enjoy the soft breezes and romantic atmosphere.